LET'S EAT
IN THE
FUNNY ZONE

Jokes, Riddles, Tongue Twisters & "Daffynitions"

By Gary Chmielewski

Illustrated by Jim Caputo

Read Jokes. Write Jokes.

NORWOOD HOUSE PRESS

A Note to Parents and Caregivers:

As the old saying goes, "Laughter is the best medicine." It's true for reading as well. Kids naturally love humor, so why not look to their interests to get them motivated to read? The Funny Zone series features books that include jokes, riddles, word plays, and tongue twisters—all of which are sure to delight your young reader.

We invite you to share this book with your child, taking turns to read aloud to one another, practicing timing, emphasis, and expression. You and your child can deliver the jokes in a natural voice, or have fun creating character voices and exaggerating funny words. Be sure to pause often to make sure your child understands the jokes. Talk about what you are reading and use this opportunity to explore new vocabulary words and ideas. Reading aloud can help your child build confidence in reading.

Along with being fun and motivating, humorous text involves higher order thinking skills that support comprehension. Jokes, riddles, and word plays require us to explore the creative use of language, develop word and sound recognition, and expand vocabulary.

At the end of the book there are activities to help your child develop writing skills. These activities tap your child's creativity by exploring numerous types of humor. Children who write materials based on the activities are encouraged to send them to Norwood House Press for publication on our website or in future books. Please see page 24 for details.

Above all, the most important part of the reading experience is to have fun and enjoy it!

Sincerely,

Shannon Cannon

Shannon Cannon
Literacy Consultant

NORWOOD HOUSE PRESS

P.O. Box 316598 • Chicago, Illinois 60631
For information regarding Norwood House Press, please visit our website at:
www.norwoodhousepress.com or call 866-565-2900.

Designer: Design Lab
Project Management: Editorial Directions

Library of Congress Cataloging-in-Publication Data:
Chmielewski, Gary, 1946–
    Let's eat in the funny zone / by Gary Chmielewski : illustrated by Jim Caputo.
        p. cm. — (The funny zone)
    Summary: "Book contains 100 food-themed jokes, tongue twisters and "Daffynitions". Backmatter includes creative writing information and exercises written by a former Harvard University Early Literacy professor. After completing the exercises, the reader is encouraged to write their own jokes and submit them for future Funny Zone titles. Full-color illustrations throughout"—Provided by publisher.
    ISBN-13: 978-1-59953-181-6 (library edition : alk. paper)
    ISBN-10: 1-59953-181-X (library edition : alk. paper) 1. Food—Juvenile humor. I. Caputo, Jim. II. Title.
PN6231.F66C46 2008
818'.5402—dc22   2007040672

Manufactured in the United States of America

LET'S EAT

What do you call cheese that isn't yours?
Nacho cheese.

What kind of dog does a person bite?
A hot dog!

What did the mother ghost tell the baby ghost when he ate too fast?
"Stop *goblin* your food!"

What did the hungry computer eat?
Chips, one byte at a time.

What did the bad chicken lay?
A deviled egg.

What did one knife say to the others?
"Let's look sharp."

What do you serve that you cannot eat?
A tennis ball.

3

The diet virus is the newest computer virus to watch out for—the computer quits after just one byte!

What is a pretzel's favorite dance?
The twist.

What do skeletons say before they start to eat?
"Bone appetit!"

What do Hungarian monsters eat?
Ghoul-lash!

What kind of nuts always seem to have a cold?
Cashews.

Why is it so easy to weigh fish?
They have their own scales.

A man in the butcher shop is 6 feet tall and wears size 11 shoes. What does he weigh?
Meat.

What's the worst thing about being an octopus?
Washing your hands before dinner.

How many hamburgers can you eat on an empty stomach?
One. After that your stomach is no longer empty!

DRINK UP!

SOUR PUSS
A cat that drinks lemonade!

What is a witch's favorite drink?
Tea-he-he-he!

Where does an alien get its milk?
The Milky Way!

Why did the man stare at the can of orange juice?
It said "concentrate."

What starts with a "t," ends with a "t," and is filled with "t"?
A teapot.

Why should a skeleton drink eight glasses of milk a day?
Milk is good for your bones!

BREAKFAST

How can you tell if a vampire has been to a bakery?

All the jelly has been sucked out of the doughnuts!

Maria: "Do you have to make so much noise when you eat?"
Darrell: "Teacher told us to start the day with a sound breakfast!"

What kind of nut has no shell?
A dough-nut.

In which country was the doughnut made?
Greece.

What happens when you tell an egg a joke?
It cracks up.

When do ghosts eat cereal?
In the *moaning*!

Why did the pig go into the kitchen?
It felt like bakin'!

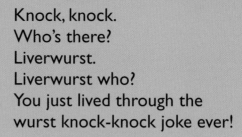

Knock, knock.
Who's there?
Liverwurst.
Liverwurst who?
You just lived through the
wurst knock-knock joke ever!

Did you ever wonder ...
... what was the best thing before sliced bread?

What do you get when you cross an
elephant and some peanut butter?
Either peanut butter that never forgets or an
elephant that sticks to the roof of your mouth!

Why don't you starve in a desert?
Because of all the sand which is there!

Jack: "Can I have a dollar
for a sandwich?"
Jill: "If you like, but it probably
won't taste very good!"

DINNER

I never smelled a smelt
that smelled as bad
as that smelt smelled.

"Jimmy, did you say your prayers before dinner?"
"No, my mom is a good cook!"

What did the pork chop say to the steak?
"It's nice to meat you."

What has four legs, a head, and leaves?
A dining-room table.

What did the hamburger name his daughter?
Patty.

Why is monastery food so greasy?
It's all cooked by friars!

What is the best way to eat spaghetti?
First, open your mouth …!

What country can't get enough to eat?
Hungary!

What country helps you cook?
Greece!

Why didn't the boy fix dinner?
He was always told, "If it ain't broke, don't fix it!"

Chris: "What should I serve with my meat loaf?"
Danita: "The antidote!"

How do you keep your dog from begging at the table?
Let him taste your cooking!

What are two things you cannot eat for supper?
Breakfast and lunch.

What do astronauts eat for dinner?
Launch meat!

VEGETABLES

What kind of tables do people eat?
Vegetables.

How do you repair a broken tomato?
Tomato paste.

Why did the other vegetables like the corn?
She was always willing to lend an ear!

Why was the mushroom the hit of the party?
He was a fungi!

What room can no one enter?
A mushroom!

How did the farmer mend his pants?
With cabbage patches.

Why can't the magician practice her new tricks in the garden?
Because the corn has ears and the potatoes have eyes.

What's the ratio of the pumpkin's circumference to its diameter?
Pumpkin Pi!

Why should potatoes be neater?
They have eyes to see what they're doing!

Why did the lettuce blush?
It saw the salad dressing.

Why doesn't the corn like the farmer?
He picks their ears.

What do you get when you drop a pumpkin?
Squash!

13

**How do you mend a
smashed pumpkin?**
A pumpkin patch!

**Take off my skin and I won't cry,
but you will. What am I?**
An onion.

**If a carrot and a cabbage
ran a race, which would win?**
The cabbage, because it's a head.

FRUITY-TOOTY

Why did the strawberry cross the road?
Because his mother was in a jam!

When do you go at red and stop at green?
When you're eating a ripe watermelon.

What is a twin's favorite food?
Pears.

Did you hear the joke about the watermelon?
It's pitiful.

Why did the banana go to the doctor?
It wasn't peeling well.

Knock, knock.
Who's there?
Cantaloupe.
Cantaloupe who?
Cantaloupe, I'm already married!

RAISIN
A worried grape.

What fruit was a great conqueror?
Alexander the Grape.

What did the grape say when the elephant sat on it?
Nothing, it just let out a little wine!

What goes up as a fruit and comes down as a vegetable?
A tomato—throw it up and it comes down a squash.

How do you get the water in watermelon?
Plant it in the spring!

What is a vampire's favorite fruit?
Necktarines!

If you were to take two apples from three apples, how many would you have?
Two—the two apples you took.

ON THE SIDE

Why was the margarine unhappy when she met the marmalade?
She was expecting something butter!

What stays hot no matter how cold it gets?
Pepper.

Knock, knock.
Who's there?
Butter.
Butter who?
Butter late than never!

Why does the toast like the knife best?
Because the knife butters him up!

What did the cucumber say to the vinegar?
"Well, this is a fine pickle you've gotten us into!"

What happens when a hamburger misses a lot of school?
He has a lot of *ketchup* time.

Why did the boy throw butter out his window?
He wanted to see a butterfly!

What did the mayonnaise say to the refrigerator?
"Close the door! Can't you see I'm dressing?"

Mother: "Lisa, have you finished filling up the salt shaker?"
Lisa: "No, mom. It's hard pushing the salt through those tiny holes!"

19

SWEETS

Why did the pie crust go to the dentist?
It needed a filling!

Double bubble gum bubbles double.

Why did the cow eat a chocolate bar?
She wanted to make chocolate milk.

Lisa: "Would you like some Egyptian pie?"
Tina: "What's Egyptian pie?"
Lisa: "You know, it's the kind our mummy used to bake."

What's the best thing to put into a pie?
Your teeth.

What does a monster chew?
Boo-ble gum!

How do you make a milkshake?
Creep up behind a cow and say "BOO"!

Emily: "I can always tell when it's time for a snack."
Dave: "How?"
Emily: "My big hand is on the cookie jar and my little hand is inside!"

LAYERCAKE
A cake that makes its own eggs.

What kind of keys do children like to carry?
Cookies.

What kind of plant do you put in a cake?
Flower!

What's a vampire's favorite candy?
Sucker!

Why did the cookie go to the emergency room?
It felt crummy.

What dessert do you get when eating in the school cafeteria?
Stomach-cake.

Which candy can't get anywhere on time?
Chocolate!

Which burns longer, the candles on a girl's birthday cake, or the candles on a boy's birthday cake?
Neither—they both burn shorter.

21

EATING OUT

What does a ghost order in an Italian restaurant?
Spook-ghetti!

What is the best day to have your cookout?
Fry-day

What did the cannibal order for takeout?
A pizza with everyone on it.

Customer: "Waiter, my vegetables just punched me!"
Waiter: "That's because they're black-eyed peas!"

A man walked into a restaurant.
"Do you serve crabs here?" he asked the waiter.
"We serve anyone," replied the waiter. "Sit right down!"

Louis: "What is this insect in my soup?"
Waiter: "I wish you wouldn't ask me. I don't know one bug from another!"

Why did the man eat at the bank?
He wanted to eat rich food.

Tony: "Waiter, will my pizza be long?"
Waiter: "No sir, it will be round."

Tina: "Waiter, this food tastes kind of funny."
Waiter: "Then why aren't you laughing?"

WRITING JOKES CAN BE AS MUCH FUN AS READING THEM!

Tongue twisters are a common type of joke. A tongue twister is a phrase that is hard to say because all or most of the words begin with the same letter or repeat a similar sound. This is called alliteration.

When a bunch of words in a row share a similar sound, the speaker often can't pronounce them properly. His or her tongue gets "twisted." Here is a tongue twister from page 10:

> I never smelled a smelt
> that smelled as bad
> as that smelt smelled.

Not only is this tongue twister funny because it is difficult to say without messing up, it also makes use of a pun (a joke based on a word that means more than one thing or two words that sound the same but have different meanings). A smelt is a type of fish with a particular smell, but it also sounds a lot like *smelled*.

YOU TRY IT!

All it takes to make a hilarious tongue twister is a little creativity and patience. Try to come up with some, either by yourself or with some friends.

Start by making a list of your favorite foods or snacks. Think about how the words sound and what letter they begin with.

Now get writing: think of goofy sentences to write about the words you came up with. Make sure that you choose words that begin with the same letter or have similar sounds. Here's an example for the word *tuna*:

> Tina taste tested a ton of tuna for Tanya.

Once everyone has written a tongue twister, try and see who can say the most tongue twisters three times in a row without messing up. And remember, tongue twisters are meant to be silly, so have fun!

SEND US YOUR JOKES!

Pick out the best tongue twister that you created and send it to us at Norwood House Press. We will publish it on our website — organized according to grade level, the state you live in, and your first name.

Selected jokes might also appear in a future special edition book, *Kids Write in the Funny Zone*. If your joke is included in the book, you and your school will receive a free copy.

Here's how to send the jokes to Norwood House Press:

1) Go to www.norwoodhousepress.com.
2) Click on the **Enter the Funny Zone** tab.
3) Select and print the joke submission form.
4) Fill out the form, include your joke, and send to:
> The Funny Zone
> Norwood House Press
> PO Box 316598
> Chicago, IL 60631

Here's how to see your joke posted on the website:

1) Go to www.norwoodhousepress.com.
2) Click on the **Enter the Funny Zone** tab.
3) Select **Kids Write in the Funny Zone** tab.
4) Locate your grade level, then state, then first name.
> If it's not there yet check back again.